Courtroom Prayers for Beginners: A Complete Guide to Courts of Heaven Prayers

Pius Joseph © Text 2020

All rights Reserved.

or mechanical methods, without the prior written permission of the publisher

Except in the case of brief quotations embodied in critical reviews and certain other noncommercial uses permitted by copyright law.

The author is aware that the application of this book may differ from one person to another as such things as faith, persistence, trust, and love for God can determine the outcomes that you receive from the application of the principles in this book.

Unless otherwise indicated, all scriptural quotations are taken from the King James Version © 1988-2007 Bible Soft Inc.

Scripture marked GWT is taken from GOD'S WORD Copyright © 1995 by God's Word to the Nations Bible Society. All rights reserved.

TABLE OF CONTENTS

CHAPTER 1

The scriptural basis for the Courts of Heaven

Before delving into the scriptural basis of the courts of heaven, let me explain what a court is. A court is a place where cases are heard and justice is administered between disputing parties. A courtroom is a particular place where this administration of justice takes place.

Though this may seem needless to some people, I feel obligated to give this definition so that we can have a perspective of what we are going to be dealing with in the Book.

In April 2020, I received an email from a brother after publishing my book, Prayers That Open the Courts of Heaven. He wrote me an interesting email whose contents I will quote below. To protect his privacy, I won't state his name or the country he is from.

> *About the Courts of Heaven, I am a bit skeptical and scared too. It is a new theology for me and messes with my view of God. Is God dependent upon our help to inform him about our needs and help him to bring breakthrough to us when he is the highest priest of all times and for all eternity?*

I have read your other book about this topic, too, but I will surely give it a try...

Well, brother, I hope you are reading this book right now. I also want to thank you for your email because it strengthened my resolve to write the beginners guide to courtroom prayers. If not that you have written to me, I won't have known that some people have doubts concerning the courtroom prayer. I will use Scriptures to show the foundational basis for courtroom prayer and why it is not a new theology at all. The fact that many do not employ the use of the courtroom prayer for their benefits, does not make it of non-effects. Courtroom prayer remains one of the easiest ways to get your answers when situations are stubborn or when they are proving difficult to deal with. Let us look at it from the biblical basis of Scriptures because anything that has a Bible reference, is worth the practice.

Isaiah 43:25-28

> *I alone am the one who is going to wipe away your rebellious actions*
> *for my own sake.*
> *I will not remember your sins anymore.*
> *26 Remind me of what happened.*
> *Let us argue our case together.*
> *State your case so that you can prove you are right.*

(GWT)

This scripture in Isaiah captures the very essence of the court system itself. The scriptures say state your case and prove that you are right. This speaks of a court system. Although other versions of the Bible talk about pleading your cause, it doesn't take out the essence of that scripture. It still indicates that it is a court system that you will use to plead your cause before the Lord.

Cases are proved in a court of law. A party will do that through the abundance of evidence before the jury or judge. He will then persuade the court that he was right and the other party was wrong. That is essentially what the Scripture is talking about for you to prove that you are right.

From the above Scripture, courtroom prayer has a scriptural basis and since it does then it must be something that we could practice. When you have pleaded your cause before the court, then a judgement would be entered in your favour stating that you are justified. By the scripture, this particular thing isn't permitted to happen. You are justified by the decree that is going to be issued in your favour against whatever that you may have been going through. So what we are dealing with here is a typical court system. When a person goes and plead his cause and say whether, by the provision of the word of God, this is supposed to happen to me or not, he is employing the use of the court system.

Daniel 7:9-10

> *I watched until thrones were set up*
> *and the Ancient One, who has lived for endless years, sat down.*
> *His clothes were as white as snow*
> *and the hair on his head was like pure wool.*
> *His throne was fiery flames, and its wheels were burning fire.*
> *10 A river of fire flowed. It came from him.*
> *Thousands and thousands served him.*

> *Ten thousand times ten*
> *thousand were stationed in*
> *front of him.*
> *The court convened,*
> *and the books were opened.*

(GWT)

This scripture also typifies a court system where God sits on his throne and judgment given. The Bible says books were opened and judgment was going to be according to what is contained on the pages of these books. On earth, judgment is usually given in a court system and not anywhere else. Again this scripture shows that what we are dealing with is a court system before the throne of God.

Psalms 82:1-3

> *God takes his place in his*
> *own assembly.*
> *He pronounces judgment*
> *among the gods:*

2 "How long are you going to judge unfairly?
How long are you going to side with wicked people?"
Selah
3 Defend weak people and orphans.
Protect the rights of the oppressed and the poor.

This is a psalm, but the theme running across that scripture portrays a court system where God does justice to the afflicted. Who are those who are afflicted? Of course, this would mean any child of God who is going through any unpleasant situation of life that God has not ordained. God would do justice to the affliction that the believer has been going through. This shows that a court is required for this justice to be done. This is a strong reason why we should hold onto the court system as a means by which God can do justice to his children and enter judgement in favour of his elect. Once something has a scriptural basis, then there is a strong reason that we should practice that act.

Revelation 6:10

> *And they cried with a loud voice, saying, How long, O Lord, holy and true, dost thou not judge and avenge our blood on them that dwell on the earth?*

The scripture under reference also shows God is going to judge the earth. The redeemed of the Lord were calling on the Lord to come and render judgment in the favour of God's people.

When we are speaking about the courts of heaven prayers or courtroom prayers, it is not an extra-scriptural revelation. That people don't practice it doesn't render it useless or unbiblical.

CHAPTER 2

Features of the Courts

Every conventional court that you see has features. The moment you step into the court, certain things are visible for you to see. We will x-ray some of the features of the courts on earth and contrast them with the Courts of Heaven. One thing is worthy of note here that whatever we see here on earth is a shadow of what is in heaven. God gave revelation to the scientists or to people to be able to bring down the heavenly dimension to the earth.

The Judge

In a normal functioning court, there is a judge. He has the responsibility of directing the affairs of the court. The judge decides to choose which case is to be heard first. It is also his decision to determine which of the witnesses of the parties should testify first.

Depending on the length of the case, all the parties will be required to appear in court when necessary during the pendency of the case and the judge determines what happens during that time. After the evidence of the parties, the judge will give his judgement in favour of one of the parties before him. And whatever decision that the judge gives, will be binding on all the parties whether they are at peace with the decision or not. They would have no choice but to obey whatever decision or direction that the judge gives after the case. The parties have brought the matter before the judge and whatever decision that the judge gives will bind them.

In the Courts of Heaven, there is also a judge. And it is God who sits to administer justice to all who appear before the Courts of Heaven. When the believers have presented their situation before the throne, God will decide based on the standard of his word whether the believer is entitled to the grant of the petition that has been brought before the throne.

Hebrews 12:23

> *To the general assembly and church of the firstborn, which are written in heaven, and to God the Judge of all, and to the spirits of just men made perfect,*

John 5:22

> *For the Father judgeth no man, but hath committed all judgment unto the Son:*

All the above Scriptures point to one clear fact that God is the judge. And just as you have a judge in the conventional court system on earth, that is how you have a judge in the courts of heaven. He is the one that will enter judgement in the favour of any believer that appears before him when the believer has presented copious evidence that this affliction is not permitted to remain in his life based on the law books of God, the Holy Bible. Upon hearing what the believer has presented before the courts of heaven, God will enter a judgement which will either bind the devil or the spirit that is responsible for the affliction which the believer has been subjected to. It is, therefore, necessary to be able to know the word because courtroom prayer is anchored on the word of God.

And whenever God, the greatest judge has determined any matter that the believer has brought before him, the matter remains solved with finality. So the administration of justice in the courts of heaven is what God does.

The Attorney

The practice of law is a specialised field which is why lawyers have to go through a rigorous training for many years for them to qualify to be admitted into the bar for the practice of their profession. Without these professionals who help parties to conduct their cases in line with the rules of the law, it will be impossible for any court of law to function. So you see the lawyer plays an important role in any judicial system. The success or failure of the case is dependent on the type of lawyer that a litigant picks. Pick a good lawyer who knows what he's doing, and you will win your case. Pick a bad lawyer who does not know the law, and he will ruin your case.

We also have a specialised advocate in the courts of heaven who has been trained in matters of all types of advocacy.

Hebrews 5:8-9

> *Though he were a Son, yet learned he obedience by the things which he suffered;*
> *9 And being made perfect, he became the author of eternal salvation unto all them that obey him;*

The name of that advocate is called Jesus, the Prince of peace. He is our lawyer before the courts of heaven. For God to ensure that he knows how to administer the justice system of heaven, he sent him down to earth to die on the cross of Calvary. No wonder the Bible says in the book of Hebrews, that we have an advocate who had been tempted in the same way that we have yet without sin.

Hebrews 4:15

> *15 For we have not an high priest which cannot be touched with the feeling of*

our infirmities; but was in all points tempted like as we are, yet without sin.

He has been practising advocacy even before the foundation of the earth was ever laid. By his divinity and power, he can help everyone who appears before the court of heaven win his case.

The Bible tells us in the book of 1 John 2:1-2:

> *My little children, these things write I unto you, that ye sin not. And if any man sin, we have an advocate with the Father, Jesus Christ the righteous:*
> *2 And he is the propitiation for our sins: and not for ours only, but also for the sins of the whole world.*

The Scripture tells us that Jesus is our lawyer before the courts of heaven. So whenever you appear before the courts, you already have someone who is advocating for you.

1 Timothy 2:5

> *For there is one God, and one mediator between God and men, the man Christ Jesus;*

If it is a satanic infirmity that you have brought before the courts of heaven so that the spirit responsible for that affliction may be judged, it is the advocate that will insist that based on what I have done on the cross of cavalry, this son or daughter of mine is not supposed to experience this affliction and that the court ought to grant the order restraining the devil from further afflicting the believer in question.

In the book of Zechariah, God was speaking to the high priest Joshua which in Hebrew is Yeshua, meaning Jesus.

Zechariah 3:7

Thus saith the Lord of hosts; If thou wilt walk in my ways, and if thou wilt keep my charge, then thou shalt also judge my house, and shalt also keep my courts, and I will give thee places to walk among these that stand by.

As long as Jesus continues to walk in the commandment of his Father, God has given him the power to keep his courts. It is a duty that Jesus has been doing and will continue to do as our advocate in heaven. So the lawyer we are talking about is not just a mere lawyer or a quack that you will be afraid of entrusting him with your case. He's very versed in the administration of spiritual and physical matters that concern the life of a believer on the earth. When you make any petition before the throne in the Courts of Heaven during a courtroom prayer, it is Jesus who will plead and advocate with the Father why your petition should not only be heard but also granted too. Anyone who has ever gone to the courts of heaven and came out with a prayer answered, or a decree restraining the works of darkness or even a judgement that has been entered in his favour, was able to do so only because Jesus, the lawyer, advocated that his petition should be granted. Without his activities in the Courts of Heaven, most courtroom prayers will return unanswered.

You have nothing to fear whenever you go before the courts of heaven for a courtroom prayer because a special advocate is there as your lawyer. He is very experienced in matters of the law because he has been doing this for all of eternity. Right from the time of Adam, to our present dispensation, this lawyer has been advocating for us. So you aren't dealing with the lawyer who does not know what he's doing. This lawyer is a rare one with a huge experience spanning through several eternal ages. He is a type of lawyer that you can give him your case and go to sleep, knowing that he will apply the facts (the matter that is bothering you) and the law, the Holy Bible for your sole benefit to ensure that you get a favourable outcome from your courtroom prayers.

Friends, have you ever looked at this Scripture and consider it very deeply – 1 John 5:14-15:

> *And this is the confidence that we have in him, that, if we ask any thing according to his will, he heareth us:*
> *15 And if we know that he hear us, whatsoever we ask, we know that we have the petitions that we desired of him.*

If you have considered that Scripture very well you will understand one thing from it. That we have confidence in him and whenever we come before him with our petition, he hears and answers. Why do we have such a level of confidence in him? It is quite simple. There is an advocate who stands in the Courts of Heaven pleading with God why our petition should always be granted. Even though it may not be a courtroom prayer, whenever you pray on any subject matter, it is our lawyer, the advocate who pleads your cause before the throne so that God grants you what you are asking for.

This accounts for the reason why our prayers will have no basis without the name of Jesus. Even when Jesus was on earth, he told the disciples to ask in his name, and it will be granted. How beautiful it is to have an advocate in the person of Jesus.

Witnesses

Ever stepped into a courtroom before? If you have, you would have seen witnesses testifying on behalf of one of the parties to support his or her case. An eyewitness is any person who has seen the event happened or who have some knowledge about the case in court and could testify in support of one of the parties before it. In every court proceedings, witnesses are required to strengthen the case of one of the parties. If you ask some lawyers, they will tell you that there are certain types of cases that without witnesses, your chances of succeeding are very slim. Do you see how important witnesses are to cases in court? Their presence or absence can mar the success of any case.

The above description of the physical court system is true of the spiritual as well. In the Courts of Heaven, there are also witnesses. I'm going to show you three of the powerful witnesses you have in support of your case. And you know what, these witnesses are there to testify on your behalf.

The Bible tells us that there are three that bear witnesses in heaven – the Father, the Son, and the Spirit.

1 John 5:7

For there are three that bear witness in heaven: the Father, the Word, and the Holy Spirit; and these three are one.

(NKJV)

1 John 5:8

And there are three that bear witness on earth: the Spirit, the water, and the blood; and these three agree as one.

So the three that bear witness in heaven, are the Father, the Son, and the Spirit. These are the three witnesses that will be working in your favour in the Courts of Heaven. They are the witnesses that will testify on your behalf. You see the reason why the courts of heaven prayer are one of the best ways to pray to handle difficult situations? The godhead is heavily involved in the Courts of Heaven.

I want you to pay attention to the second verse of the Scripture we have quoted above. While the Father, the Son, and the Spirit bear witness in heaven, when it comes to the matters of the earth, two principal personalities bear that witness. The Bible tells us that, the spirit, the water, and the blood. It is needful to explain why the Bible uses the spirit and the water. The spirit that the Bible is referring to is the Holy Spirit, the helper that God has sent into the life of every believer. Water used in the Scripture is also the spirit showing us that whatever the spirit says it must be confirmed. In this passage, the Holy Spirit is represented by a symbolic means – water. You would see in Scripture that the Holy Spirit is sometimes represented through the symbol of water.

John 7:37-39

> *In the last day, that great*
> *day of the feast, Jesus stood*
> *and cried, saying, If any man*

thirst, let him come unto me, and drink.

38 He that believeth on me, as the scripture hath said, out of his belly shall flow rivers of living water.

39 (But this spake he of the Spirit, which they that believe on him should receive: for the Holy Ghost was not yet given; because that Jesus was not yet glorified.)

We know about the dove, we also know about fire and the wind. All these are symbolic representations of the Holy Spirit. The blood that is used in the Scripture is speaking about Jesus, who shed his blood on the cross of Calvary that you and I may receive the life of God. Whenever you come before the Courts of Heaven for a courtroom prayer, two personalities are eyewitnesses of what happened on the earth: the Holy Spirit and Jesus himself. When you are petitioning your request for an order against the works of darkness, the Holy Spirit and Jesus would be saying, I was there when the affliction came, and I can bear witness to all that happened.

So the Holy Spirit and Jesus are the ones who will bear witness to the event. They are your witness when you come before the Courts of Heaven concerning the event that led to your petition.

I believe by now you should begin to notice something very important here, that one person doubles both as a witness and as an advocate when it comes to the courts of heaven prayers. Jesus Christ! He's both our advocate and lawyer before the courts of heaven, and he also serves as a witness who saw the event or the affliction you went through. How beautiful the Courts of Heaven prayers is!

Besides the above which you will see in a conventional courtroom process, there are other things that you will see when you enter into a courtroom. You will see a gavel, other people who might be interested in the case, and even journalists who came to witness what happened so that they can tell the story in the media.

In the courts of heaven too, there are other things that you will see. Let's look at them very briefly.

You will see the throne of God

In the same way that you see a judge sits in court to administer justice to all those who appear before him, that is the same way that God sits on the throne to administer justice to all those who bring petitions in the Courts of Heaven. The only difference between his throne and that of an earthly judge is that righteousness and justice are the foundation of the throne of God. He doesn't just issue a courtroom order anyhow or just because the believer appeared before him for a courtroom prayer.

There must be a justifiable reason based on the justice system of heaven, and the word of God for God to make any declaration in the courtroom. You know what my friends, the word of God is one of the strongest justifiable reasons why an order will be made in the favour of a believer.

Angels

The Bible tells us something important in the book of Revelation that there are angels before the throne that sing, holy, holy, holy is the Lord God Almighty (Revelation 4:8). These angels may be performing some functions in the courtroom. Unlike the courts we see here on the earth, you will never see someone singing in the courtroom for any reason. If a person begins to sing before a judge, he could be cited for contempt of court because his songs may constitute a nuisance to the ongoing proceedings before the court.

Conversely, the Courts of Heaven is not so. Some angels have the constant assignment of worshipping God. As long as you go before the Courts of Heaven, worship is a continual thing you will experience there. The angels are constantly singing, holy, holy, holy! We will discuss the issue of worship in the subsequent chapters of this book as it is an important factor when you come before the Courts of Heaven. It is a protocol that should be observed whenever you have gained access to the courts of heaven where your courtroom prayer is offered.

Bailiffs of Courts

The bailiff of the court is anyone who is saddled with the responsibility of carrying out certain types of order of the court. It could be minor assignment such as serving court processes and ensuring that orders given by the court are served on the party concerned. And who are those who carry out these orders in the courtroom of heaven? They are the angels of God. Although they do not constitute a part of the courts of heaven, you will see them there because they carry out some assignments for God.

Luke 1:19

> *And the angel answering said unto him, I am Gabriel, that stand in the presence of God; and am sent to speak unto thee, and to shew thee these glad tidings.*

When the angel Gabriel appeared to Zechariah in the temple, he told Zachariah that I am Gabriel that stands in the presence of God. And by the standing, I have been sent to deliver this message to you. So angels stand before the presence of the LORD to carry out different assignments that God would require them to do.

The Registrar of the Court

The registrar of the court is an integral part of the court system, and he is responsible for calling the cases to be dealt with in any particular proceedings. Any time you go to court and you hear someone calling, the state versus so so and so, it is usually the registrar of the court that performs that function. And when it comes to the courtroom session which a believer might have initiated to deal with stubborn situations or difficulty that the enemy has thrown around his life, the angels of the Lord are the registrars of the court.

We have already seen in the Scripture that angels are before the throne to carry out assignments that God wants them to perform. Calling out cases to be dealt with is the responsibility of the angels of God. The Bible tells us that they are ministering spirits sent forth to minister unto them that shall be heirs of salvation (Hebrews 1:14).

CHAPTER 3

Courtroom Terminologies

Before a lawyer ever gets to practice law, he is trained through the process of education in the law school. This may take several years before he gets himself acquainted with the legal system. There is no way that a sophomore student from Harvard can enter into the court to practice law no matter how good he may be. Even if he is one that tops his class with good grades. His intelligence in the class does not disregard the need for training at the law school.

While the lawyer is in the school, he's being taught the legal terminologies that he would need when he becomes a lawyer. Even if he knows literature very well, it won't help him until he learns the terminologies of lawyers. When he has been admitted to the bar for the practice of his profession, and he appears before the judge to begin his case, and he speaks his legal terminologies acquired through the process of training, the judge understands him even though all the others who are in the court such as litigants and spectators who came to witness the legal proceedings may not be able to comprehend what the lawyer is speaking. But the judge understands what the lawyer is saying.

In the same vein, several people are attempting to do a courtroom prayer or Courts of Heaven prayer with little or no information about the courtroom. A wise man once told me, never begin anything without gathering necessary information about that subject matter. If you want to become a good courtroom prayer warrior with a hundred per cent success rate, you also need to learn the procedure of the courtroom and how it works. And that is the intent of this book to give you all the necessary tools you need as a beginner in the courtroom prayer.

The Law Books

You might not be a lawyer, adorned with a wig, a gown, and bib striding your chest. You might not be physically wearing lawyers robe, but I'm going to tell you something very surprising. Every believer who has been saved by the blood of the Lamb is a lawyer. The modalities and practices that we adopt as believers are not different from what the lawyers do in the conventional court system. When the lawyer comes before a judge, he tries to convince the judge based on existing law why judgement should be given in favour of his clients. To succeed in this, the lawyer comes with his legal books, cases that have been decided in previous matters and insist that the judge should enter judgement in his favour based on the laws that he has cited.

And that is what you do as a believer in Jesus Christ. You rely on the laws of God and cite them before the courtroom insisting why judgement should be given in your favour by stopping the particular attack or problem that you have in your life.

In the book of Joshua 1:8, the Bible gives us a very directive instruction as follows:

> *This book of the law shall not depart out of thy mouth; but thou shalt meditate therein day and night, that thou mayest observe to do according to all that is written therein: for then thou shalt make thy way prosperous, and then thou shalt have good success.*

God knows that if we allow the book of the law to depart out of our mouths, we no longer meditate on it, the courts of heaven and courtroom prayer will remain a mirage. If you hire a lawyer, and he comes to court to defend you against an allegation and the lawyer couldn't cite a single law or a section of the Constitution of the United States of America to defend you, and because of his inability to use the law you lost the case. Will you say in your opinion that the lawyer is competent? Will you be happy with the way that the lawyer conducted your case?

The next time you have another matter, would you go to the same lawyer? I will allow you to answer these questions. But if I am the one, the last time I ever stepped into his office, shall be the last because I do not regard him as a competent lawyer. How can the lawyer claim to be one without knowing the law? He is not different from someone who studied literature at the University and got a college degree.

What makes a lawyer different is his ability to use the law as a weapon to get what he wants for his clients. If he fails to be able to use the principles of the law well, his client's case can be severely damaged except it is remedied by an appeal. Even in the case of an appeal, it is not going to be a fresh case. The court of appeal will hear what the other courts heard and not something new. This singular damage was caused as a result of the inability of the lawyer to use the law well.

In the same manner, from the day that you got saved as a believer, you have become a lawyer. And your law book is the Bible. It is what governs all spiritual laws that you can see around you. And you know what, the spiritual supersedes the physical. Once anything has been effectively dealt within the realm of the spirit, it has been handled in the realm of the physical as well. God spoke in the spirit, let there be light. And there was light in the physical. So the elements of the spiritual are stronger than the elements of the physical.

Whenever lawyers are in court arguing a matter, it will intrigue you. You will keep hearing section this and section that. You will also be hearing based on the case of so so so Verse so so so, the judge must do this or do that. It is the same thing that you do when you are before the courts of heaven for a courtroom prayer. You are simply telling God, who is the judge that these are what you stated in your law book, the Holy Bible, this is permitted to happen. Or this particular attack that I am going through must be restrained.

To come before the courtroom of heaven without adequate knowledge of the law books, the Holy Bible upon which all courtroom prayer is based, is it a time wasted effort. It is necessary to state that it is here that some courtroom prayers are lost or results are gotten. The Bible tells us that let the word of God dwell in our lives richly.

Colossians 3:16

> *Let the word of Christ dwell in you richly in all wisdom; teaching and admonishing one another in psalms and hymns and spiritual songs, singing with grace in your hearts to the Lord.*

You must be a student of the Bible to be successful in courtroom prayer. I mean, you must know the word of God. It is through the word of God that you know what is permitted and what isn't permitted to happen to you. All your legal rights as a believer in Jesus Christ are clearly stated in the law books of God, the Holy Bible.

If your Bible has been covered in dust, it is time to repent from this attitude of not studying the word. If you fail to open the word and study it for your spiritual edification, you will be like that attorney we have cited in the example above who appeared before a judge and did not know what to do. As a result of the poor consultation of his legal books and the law, he damaged the case of his clients.

Even the procedures of the courtroom prayer you won't be able to use them effectively because you do not know the word of God. Recently, I did a courtroom prayer on an issue that was bothering my life. Before I began the courtroom prayer, I subjected myself to the cleansing power of the blood of Jesus. The issue of applying the blood before a courtroom prayer is what will be the subject of the next chapter. Immediately, I saw a vision. I saw the Lord Jesus took me to a pool full of blood. I entered into it, and I was soaked in the blood. When I came out, I followed him to a particular place. When we got to that place, I stopped and Jesus went ahead and sat on the throne. In the vision, I understood that I was at the gates of the courtroom. So I had to follow another procedure to be able to go beyond the gates and get into the courts, we will discuss some of these procedures in the subsequent chapters of this book. I was able to have access to the courts of heaven, and I offered some worship. I finished and made my petition before the Lord.

I was able to understand these procedures because I know what the word of God says concerning courts of heaven prayer. If I didn't know it, I will tell you that I would have failed in the courtroom prayer because I won't have known what to do to gain access into the courts where my prayer is to be offered.

The knowledge of the word of God for a believer is an indispensable tool in the Courts of Heaven prayers. If you are not acquainted with the word of God, courtroom prayer will be a great difficulty. If you are someone who knows the word of God, you will find courtroom prayer procedures easy to follow. And the choice is yours to decide from now on how successful you will be in the Courts of Heaven prayers.

CHAPTER 4

Four Steps to Enter into the Courts of Heaven

If you pray a courtroom prayer in any other place other than the Courts of Heaven, is not different from a conventional prayer and your situation can remain the same. Courtroom prayers are offered in the Courts of Heaven. If they are offered in any other place, it wouldn't give it the colour of the courtroom prayer even if the person observed some protocols of the courtroom prayer. You want to offer a courtroom prayer, you must gain entrance into the Courts of

Heaven. I want to show you a step-by-step approach of how to enter into the Courts of Heaven where your courtroom prayers are to be said.

The Step of the Blood

There is nothing that puts you away from the Courts of Heaven like sin and iniquity. The Bible tells us in the book of Habakkuk, that the eyes of the Lord are too holy to behold iniquity:

Habakkuk 1:13

> *Thou art of purer eyes than to behold evil, and canst not look on iniquity: wherefore lookest thou upon them that deal treacherously, and holdest thy tongue when the wicked devoureth the man that is more righteous than he?*

If the eyes of the Lord are too holy to behold iniquity, is it possible for that same iniquity to come into his courts? As mighty as the love that God has for Adam and Eve when they decided to embrace iniquity and sin, he stopped visiting them in the cool of the evening in the Garden of Eden.

Isaiah 59:1-2

> *Behold, the Lord's hand is not shortened, that it cannot save; neither his ear heavy, that it cannot hear:*
> *2 But your iniquities have separated between you and your God, and your sins have hid his face from you, that he will not hear.*

It was the same sin that serves as a termination of their stay in the Garden of Eden.

Psalms 24:3-4

*Who shall ascend into the
hill of the Lord? or who shall
stand in his holy place?
4 He that hath clean hands,
and a pure heart; who hath
not lifted up his soul unto
vanity, nor sworn
deceitfully.*

The Bible tells us in the book of Psalms that who can ascend into his holy hills. In the subsequent verses, an answer was provided. That it is only him that has clean hands who has not lifted his hands to vanity. If a man has not embraced the way of sin and iniquity, he can enter into the Courts of Heaven.

Does that mean that anyone who has sinned or done anything wrong cannot enter into the Courts of Heaven? Well, if a believer will subject himself to the washing power of the blood of Jesus, he can still enter into the Courts of Heaven and offer his prayers there. The Bible tells us that the blood of Jesus cleanses us from all sins. The number one step for gaining access into the Courts of Heaven is to submit yourself to the cleansing power of the blood of Jesus. You plead the blood of Jesus upon your life and apply its cleansing power to your body, soul, and spirit. Once you have been washed by the blood of Jesus, your courtroom prayer will be offered without hindrance.

This number one step of courtroom prayer is highly necessary if a believer must achieve any success there. The failure to submit yourself to the washing power of the blood of Jesus will hinder the effectiveness of your courtroom prayer. Sin or iniquity is what separates man and God. Whenever God sees sin, he distances himself. Whenever God sees purity, he draws himself closer.

Even if you have been living a life of purity and you haven't committed any known sin to your knowledge, this number one step of cleansing yourself with the blood of Jesus is necessary. The Bible tells us that no one is righteous. The reason for this is simple! It is possible to entertain thoughts or said something that offended God without even knowing it. It is also possible that the Holy Spirit hasn't convicted you of that sin yet. Shortly before he does that, you rushed into the Courts of Heaven for a courtroom prayer. Do you think that the courtroom prayers will be effective when there is an issue of sin that has not been cleansed by the blood of Jesus? Sincerely, it won't!

One of the greatest tools that God has left for us on the earth to continue to help us unite with God even when we have fallen short of his glory, is the blood of Jesus. It doesn't matter the type of sin that you have committed once you can bring yourself under the washing power of the blood of Jesus. It will cleanse you and remove any hindrance that can prevent your courtroom prayer from being effective. As a beginner, never forget that before you begin to do any courtroom prayer in the Courts of Heaven, bring yourself under the washing power of the blood of Jesus. In essence, purify yourself by the blood of Jesus so that you can have full access to the Courts of Heaven.

Hebrews 10:19

> *Having therefore, brethren, boldness to enter into the holiest by the blood of Jesus,*

Releasing it Step

The next step that you need to take after pleading the blood of Jesus is to release it. Is there anyone who has sinned against you? Is there anyone who has offended you? Who is it that has done wrong to you? It is important at this stage to release the person and offer forgiveness. No amount of pleading the blood of Jesus can cleanse the sin of unforgiveness. The biblical injunction given to us for forgiveness is for us to forgive those who have wronged us.

Matthew 6:12

> *And forgive us our debts, as*
> *we forgive our debtors.*

You want God to forgive you, then forgive those who have offended you. Pleading the blood of Jesus to gain access to the courts of heaven without forgiving or releasing those who have offended you won't make the cut. In this step, you have to forgive those who have offended you.

As we forgive others their wrongs, that is how God can forgive us our wrong too. Which is the reason why the Bible says, forgive us our debts as we forgive those who trespass against us. If you have received forgiveness from God, you also have to give forgiveness to others. That is how it is. And nothing more will change it.

Matthew 18:23-35

> *Therefore is the kingdom of*
> *heaven   likened   unto   a*

certain king, which would take account of his servants.

24 And when he had begun to reckon, one was brought unto him, which owed him ten thousand talents.

25 But forasmuch as he had not to pay, his lord commanded him to be sold, and his wife, and children, and all that he had, and payment to be made.

26 The servant therefore fell down, and worshipped him, saying, Lord, have patience with me, and I will pay thee all.

27 Then the lord of that servant was moved with compassion, and loosed him, and forgave him the debt.

28 But the same servant went out, and found one of his fellowservants, which

owed him an hundred pence: and he laid hands on him, and took him by the throat, saying, Pay me that thou owest.

29 And his fellowservant fell down at his feet, and besought him, saying, Have patience with me, and I will pay thee all.

30 And he would not: but went and cast him into prison, till he should pay the debt.

31 So when his fellowservants saw what was done, they were very sorry, and came and told unto their lord all that was done.

32 Then his lord, after that he had called him, said unto him, O thou wicked servant, I forgave thee all that debt, because thou desiredst me:

33 Shouldest not thou also have had compassion on thy fellowservant, even as I had pity on thee?

34 And his lord was wroth, and delivered him to the tormentors, till he should pay all that was due unto him.

35 So likewise shall my heavenly Father do also unto you, if ye from your hearts forgive not every one his brother their trespasses.

In the Scripture above we saw the story of a man who had been forgiven by his master of the huge debt that he owed. After he had received forgiveness from his master, he went and met another person who owed him a little amount of money. He immediately demanded the payment be made quickly to him. When the debtor couldn't pay, he ordered him to be incarcerated behind bars.

It later got to the ears of his master what he had done to another person who owed him a little amount of money.

Upon hearing the act of the servant, the master immediately demanded that he should repay what he's owing too.

That is a principle of God. We have committed several wrongs and errors against him. He forgave us. And someone did something small to us and we don't want to let go. As long as we don't let go, our initial offences before God are remembered. Be it fornication, theft, lust, et cetera. That is the only circumstances in the Bible that God remembers our sin. If we do not forgive others, we bring to his remembrance all the things that we have done in the past.

As you are reading this right now, there are people that you know you need to forgive. They indeed did what badly hurt you. It is also true that what they did in your eyes was big. But you have to release forgiveness if praying in the Courts of Heaven is what you want to do now. And I know that the Holy Spirit is beginning to nudge your heart concerning people that you need to forgive. Do so quickly so that you can have access to the Courts of Heaven for your courtroom prayers. If you do not forgive, you will waste your time in the courts of heaven and no order will be given against the devil or his agents.

The step of the Psalms

Psalm 100:4

> *Enter into his gates with thanksgiving, and into his courts with praise: be thankful unto him, and bless his name.*

The Scripture under reference tells us to enter into his gates with thanksgiving and into his courts with praise. There are two things you need to do to gain access into the courts of heaven where our courtroom prayers are going to be offered.

A. Thanksgiving – As a beginner in the Courts of Heaven prayers, you need to understand this protocol. What will give you access to the gates of heaven is Thanksgiving. And there are several things to be thankful to God for. One of which is the gift of life. The air you breathe freely is being paid by some people as oxygen in the hospital. The salvation you have was given to you by Jesus Christ even though there are some people that you know who perished without knowing Jesus. The financial provision that you have been enjoying can constitute a serious focus of your thanksgiving. The health of your family that no one has fallen sick in the past year or six months, is also something that you can be thankful to God for. What is it? If you can only think deeply about the things that God has been doing for you, you will be very thankful to him. These are some of the factors that can constitute the focus of your praise to gain access into the courts of heaven where your courtroom prayers are going to be offered. If your destination is the courts of heaven, then Thanksgiving must be your starting point. You start by thanking God for all he has done for you. Anything at all that you can remember that God has done for you in the past or the present, use it to thank God. The moment you begin to thank God and you do it effectively, the gates of heaven will be opened to you. If you are travelling to Ontario and you decided to stop at Washington State, will you say in all honesty that you went to Ontario? I believe, no! Your journey will be seen as completed when you have arrived in Ontario, Canada. Your Thanksgiving is the same as the example above. Thanksgiving will take you to the gates of heaven but won't grant you access into the courts of heaven where your courtroom prayers are going to be said. To be able to gain access to the courts of heaven, you need another different step that you need to take. I will show you the next step.

B. Praise – This is the tool that takes you beyond the limits of the gates of heaven into the Courts of Heaven where your courtroom prayer is going to be carried out. After you have thanked God with the whole of your heart, the next important thing that you must do is to offer praises to God. It is your praises that will usher you into the Courts of Heaven for you to begin your courtroom prayer. This step is very necessary for a beginner to follow carefully so that he can arrive at the desired destination of the Courts of Heaven. In case you don't know what to praise God for, let me give you a small list of what you can praise the Lord for.

I. Praise God for being your saviour.

II. Praise God for the demonstration of his might in your life.

III. Praise God for the demonstration of his might and power in the lives of others.

IV. Praise God for his faithfulness in your life.

V. Praise God for being your creator.

VI. Praise God for being the creator of the universe.

VII. Praise God for the things he has created which you can see.

VIII. Praise God for the sufficiency of his power at work on the earth.

IX. Praise God for the demonstration of his might which you have seen in the Scriptures.

X. Praise God for the promises, prophecies, and every word that he has spoken over your life either personally by the revelation which you have received or through a prophet of the Lord.

These are things you can use to praise God for if you don't know what to use as the focus of your praise. The careful observance of this protocol of the Psalms will take you from the gates into the courts of heaven for your courtroom prayer.

The Step of the Holy, Holy

One of the powerful things that take place continuously in the courts of God is worship.

Revelation 4:8-11

> *And the four beasts had each of them six wings about him; and they were full of eyes within: and they rest not day and night, saying, Holy, holy, holy, Lord God Almighty, which was, and is, and is to come.*

9 And when those beasts give glory and honour and thanks to him that sat on the throne, who liveth for ever and ever,

10 The four and twenty elders fall down before him that sat on the throne, and worship him that liveth for ever and ever, and cast their crowns before the throne, saying,

11 Thou art worthy, O Lord, to receive glory and honour and power: for thou hast created all things, and for thy pleasure they are and were created.

The Scripture under reference tells us that the four beasts rest not day and night. They are before the courts of God and one of the things that take place there is constant worship. After you have pleaded the blood of Jesus, released it, observed the protocols of the Psalms, the next thing to do after you have gained entrance into the courts of heaven is to worship. There is no place you can't enter in this his life if you understand the rules, procedures, and protocols there. If you want to enter into the White House, there are procedures and protocols which you need to follow. If you follow them, you will enter the White House. If you refuse to follow them, you will never find yourself there. It is possible that before you see the president of the United States of America in the White House, you may need to book an appointment. Even with your appointment, there are things you need to do when you get to the White House before you can see Mr President. From the booking of your appointment down to the procedures you need to follow to enter into the White House, all of these can be categorised as steps you need to take or the protocols to observe to gain entrance into the White House. This is also true for courtroom prayer. All that we have outlined so far are the steps you need to take before you gain access into the Courts of Heaven. And even when you gain access into the Courts of Heaven, you still need to offer worship to God for you to offer your prayers in the courtroom.

CHAPTER 5

Praying in Tongues as a Beginner in the Courtroom

Your ability to pray in tongues is good but when it comes to courtroom prayer, it must be used wisely. A courtroom prayer which is done in the courts of heaven is like the conventional court we have on the earth. To that extent, every court where a trial is conducted has a language that the proceedings of the courts are performed. You can never go to a court in Saudi Arabia and hear them conducting their court proceedings in English when both the accused persons, the lawyers, and even the witnesses do not understand the English language.

In the unlikely event that the proceedings of the court was conducted in a foreign language unknown to the parties if you are present in the court will you say that justice was effectively done? If I was an observer on that day when the proceedings of the court were conducted in a foreign language unknown to the parties of the case, I would go out with one notion – justice was not done in this case. How can court proceedings be conducted in the language unknown to the parties and the court had to give judgement in favour of the prosecution or the state.

In the same vein, the gift of praying in tongues as good as it may be, cannot be used indiscriminately in the courtroom prayer. It must be used as led by the spirit of God. The Bible tells us in the book of 1 Corinthians 14:2, he that prays in an unknown tongue, speaks mysteries in the realm of the spirit.

1 Corinthians 14:2

> *For he that speaketh in an unknown tongue speaketh not unto men, but unto God: for no man understandeth him; howbeit in the spirit he speaketh mysteries.*

And when you are in the courtroom and you begin to speak in tongues, you are speaking mysteries. It is only the Holy Spirit, God the Father, and God the Son that understand what you are saying when you pray in tongues. Even you who is praying in tongues do not know what you are saying unless you have the gift of interpretation of tongues or the gift of interpretation of tongues was released upon you to understand what you are praying. In effect, the whole proceedings are being conducted in a mysterious language. No one understands anything you are saying unless interpreted.

If you go to the courts of heaven for a courtroom prayer, praying in the spirit or praying in tongues must be used with wisdom. Without this understanding, some believers will go to the Courts of Heaven and be praying in tongues as if the courtroom prayer they are doing is the same as the regular prayer. If you follow this approach, it is possible to come out of the courtroom with no result at all. May that never be your portion in the name of Jesus.

When you want to pray in tongues in the courtroom, it is better to state your cause or problem in understanding (maybe English or your language before praying in tongues.

1 Corinthians 14:15

> *What is it then? I will pray with the spirit, and I will pray with the understanding*

also: I will sing with the spirit, and I will sing with the understanding also.

The Holy Spirit and the Beginner in the Courtroom

Even if you haven't been to any school, the school of the Holy Spirit is what you need as a believer. Peter and some of the disciples were unlearned men, but they commanded some of the greatest educational attention of their time.

Acts 4:13

> *Now when they saw the boldness of Peter and John, and perceived that they were unlearned and ignorant men, they marvelled; and they took knowledge of them, that they had been with Jesus.*

And the reason for this is simple. They were taught and educated by the Holy Spirit. That is one of the ministries of the Holy Spirit in the life of a believer to teach the believer spiritually and physically as well. And when you begin your courtroom prayer, you will begin to recognise as you become more and more accustomed to praying the courtroom that the Holy Spirit is an indispensable personality in the courtroom. If you disregard his presence and his help, it is possible to miss some important things in the courtroom.

There is some aspect of some of the petition you are presenting before God in the Courts of Heaven which you may not have a full understanding of. Take for example someone is going through witchcraft oppression. He has fasted and prayed and nothing seemed to change. The believer finally decided to go to the courtroom to get justice against this attack of the devil. The eminent thing in the mind of the believer is to get justice against that witchcraft attack.

However, while praying in the courtroom, the Holy Spirit begins to reveal to the believer that there are some legal grounds upon which that witchcraft attack has been using to sustain what the believer is experiencing. If the Holy Spirit did not reveal that to the believer, he may think that all he needs to do is to get a restraining order against that witchcraft oppression. Do you see why the Holy Spirit is an important personality in courtroom prayer?

In the book of Romans 8:26, we are reminded of our inabilities and incapacities as human beings:

> *Likewise the Spirit also helpeth our infirmities: for we know not what we should pray for as we ought: but the Spirit itself maketh intercession for us with*

> *groanings which cannot be uttered.*

No matter how spiritual we become, those limitations can never be done away with unless we rely on the Holy Spirit. If you look at the wording of that Scripture, it says that the Holy Spirit helps our infirmities. So you see everyone has an infirmity. When I talk about infirmity in this context, I'm not referring to sickness or illnesses. What I mean and I believe what the Scripture is talking about is the limitation of being human beings and the flesh. You can never know everything. And even some of the most gifted prophets on the earth, rely on the gift of the spirit and his direction to be able to talk about mysterious things. Even with that, the Bible says that all the prophecies that they are prophesying are in part.

It is important, therefore, to be sensitive to the leading of the Holy Spirit when you are before the Courts of Heaven for a courtroom prayer. This is one thing as a beginner that you need to learn now. To ignore the leading of the Holy Spirit just because you know the protocols of getting into the courts of heaven for courtroom prayer, is to gravely limit yourself. I believe that the success of every courtroom prayer is anchored on the synergy that every believer can build with the Holy Spirit. If you are sensitive to his leading, he will tell you things that you need to handle even while in the courtroom praying about issues that are bothering your life.

Which is why a believer who is inflexible to the leading of the Holy Spirit, will find it very difficult to be able to walk with God. If you are a believer that your mind is always made on issues of life, you may be able to do a courtroom prayer but I can tell you that you won't be a hundred per cent successful.

The ministry of the Holy Spirit in the life of a believer is to teach you all things, including praying in the Courts of Heaven. The spiritual teaching is the exclusive preserve of the Holy Spirit. No man on earth has been given this privilege to teach a believer in all things. Even the pastors or the men of God that minister to you, rely on the Holy Spirit to convey messages to you. Without him, they will teach you only their understanding and that won't help you grow.

I know we are very familiar with this phrase, be led by the Holy Spirit. But I want to take my time and explain it to you. The leading of the Holy Spirit means that the Holy Spirit is taking steps and you are following after him. Or he is showing you clearly what you need to do in a particular situation. The Bible tells us in the book of John 16:13 that the Holy Spirit will not speak of himself. He will only tell you what he has heard:

> *Howbeit when he, the Spirit of truth, is come, he will guide you into all truth: for he shall not speak of himself;*

> *but whatsoever he shall*
> *hear, that shall he speak:*
> *and he will shew you things*
> *to come.*

So whatever direction that the Holy Spirit is giving you is coming directly from God. I mean the same person that you have appeared before for a courtroom prayer. So if the Holy Spirit heard, tell him that there is a legal ground upon which that witchcraft oppression is gaining expression, the Holy Spirit will speak to you about what he heard from the throne of grace. How beautiful the courtroom prayer is! You came before the courts of heaven with a particular thing in mind, yet the same judge who will enter judgement in your favour is telling you other things that are associated with the current attacks that you are facing.

If you have ignored the leading of the Holy Spirit on several occasions before, I am telling you now that this is the time to amend your ways and begin to be in alignment with the leading of the Holy Spirit. His ministry in your life if properly attended to will greatly transform your Courts of Heaven prayers.

The Greek word parakletos has been translated to mean advocate, comforter, helper, teacher, et cetera. So do not limit the ministry of the Holy Spirit to comforter alone. And do not also limit the ministry of the Holy Spirit to speaking in tongues alone. He does more than that. Even when you are before the courts of heaven for your prayers, he goes there with you. This is a spiritually true statement that the Holy Spirit does not leave the life of a believer until the work of the believer has ended on the earth.

So if you want to be a successful courtroom prayer warrior, you need to understand that that success can only be achieved with the help of the Holy Spirit. Pay attention to his leading, and you will be successful. Ignore his leading, and you won't be effective in your courtroom prayer.

CHAPTER 6

The Contempt of Court

Contempt of court is the disrespect to the authority of the court of law. When a court of law issues an order to compel the performance of an act, or direct that a particular thing should not be done and the person violates the order which was given, that is a contempt of court and a violation of the order that the court has given. It is individuals that decide to enforce contempt of court. They will come to the judge and say, what you have ordered not to be done has been done. This person has contempt for the order you've given.

Whenever you have gotten an order from the Courts of Heaven against the devil, the devil will do everything in his power to violate the order that was given by God. And whenever the devil comes after the order that God has given against him, you have to remind him that he cannot violate the order of the court that was given in the Courts of Heaven. To do that will amount to contempt of court.

It is the responsibility of the believer to remind the devil of the subsisting judgement of the Courts of Heaven. That judgement is still standing and the devil cannot violate it.

The Bible tells us that affliction is not permitted to rise again the second time.

Nahum 1:9

> *What do ye imagine against the Lord? he will make an*

*utter end: affliction shall not
rise up the second time.*

If you have gone before the courts of heaven and obtained a judgement against the spirit of infirmity, for instance, cancer. And after God has given you the judgement or order against that spirit of infirmity, and you later begin to see symptoms that had disappeared started to come back again, what the spirit of infirmity is trying to do is contempt of the Courts of Heaven. It is your responsibility as a child of God to remind the devil of the order of the courts of heaven that binds his work of darkness and that order is still standing. Use the word of God to enforce the authority of the courts over what the devil is trying to do. You tell the devil that you have already gotten an order against him so he cannot come against your health any longer.

The devil is a specialist in looking for cracks in the life of believers. He does that to ensure that whenever a believer has been delivered from an attack, he can bring the believer under his captivity again. Which is why you see people getting free today and affliction coming back tomorrow.

You resist the devil by insisting that the affliction will never come back again. Why? The Scripture says so.

The problem some believers have is not that the Bible did not say so. We are aware of what the Bible says. The challenge is when he comes back again, we forget that we have obtained an order against his work of darkness.

CHAPTER 7

How to pray in the courtroom

I want to show you some important ways of praying in the Courts of Heaven. No type of prayer in the courtroom is more superior to the other. It all depends on the need that you have and what you want the Lord to do for you.

By Petition

To petition simply is to request the Lord to do something for you. When you make a petition, you are asking God to do a particular thing for you.

1 Samuel 1:27

> *For this child I prayed; and the Lord hath given me my petition which I asked of him:*

We are all familiar with the story of Hannah how she prayed to the Lord to give her a son. After the Lord answered her prayer, Hannah recounted what she went through and stated it was a petition that the Lord had granted. This is a clear cut example of prayer by petition. And this method can be employed in the courtroom prayer as well. You can go before the Lord in the courts of heaven and make a petition of what you want him to do for you. You may have fasted over the particular issue that you have petitioned the Lord for. Your fasting did not produce results. You have also been praying over the particular issue and it seems as if your prayer wasn't producing any result either. Then you followed all the protocols in coming into the Courts of Heaven and made your petition before the Lord.

By your petition, you are telling God to give you what you are asking for. Even though the prayer of Hannah did not occur in the Courts of Heaven, that prayer represents a classic example of a petition. You are asking the Lord to do something for you. Whenever you go before the Courts of Heaven and you are making a request before the Lord, it is a petition. This is one of the ways to pray in the Courts of Heaven by making your petition known to the Lord.

Philippians 4:6-7

> *Be careful for nothing; but in every thing by prayer and supplication with thanksgiving let your requests be made known unto God.*

> *7 And the peace of God, which passeth all understanding, shall keep your hearts and minds through Christ Jesus.*

The Bible tells us not to be anxious for anything but by prayer and supplication, let us make our requests known unto God. The request here is the act of asking the Lord to do a certain thing for you.

By Intercession

To intercede is simply to pray for a person or stand in the gap for another person who requires the prayer. People go through a lot of things in life, and they may require our prayers. When we decide to take on the responsibility of praying for others, we are interceding for them.

It could be a burden that they have been experiencing or affliction that seems to defy all known solutions. They may have also prayed but no result came forth. By praying for the person, you are trying to stand in the gap on behalf of the individual who is going through a tough time. And people go through a lot of things in life they may not be able to open their mouths and tell you. But they are hurting deep down in their hearts.

Whenever you go into the Courts of Heaven and you need to intercede for someone, never forget to repent on behalf of the person. The sin in the life of the person can hinder the prayer from being effective.

Daniel 9:3-6

> *3 And I set my face unto the Lord God, to seek by prayer and supplication, with fasting, and sackcloth, and ashes:*
> *4 And I prayed unto the Lord my God, and made my confession, and said, O Lord, the great and dreadful God,*

keeping the covenant and mercy to them that love him, and to them that keep his commandments;
5 We have sinned, and have committed iniquity, and have done wickedly, and have rebelled, even by departing from thy precepts and from thy judgments:
6 Neither have we hearkened unto thy servants the prophets, which spake in thy name to our kings, our princes, and our fathers, and to all the people of the land.

We saw Daniel in the above Scripture praying for the nation of Israel and repenting on behalf of the entire nation. What Daniel was doing in the Scripture was the prayer of intercession even though it was not a courtroom type of prayer, the Scripture is still applicable. We can pray this kind of prayer of intercession for people and repent for them. We simply ask God to forgive them of their sins before we begin interceding on their behalf.

By Judgement

This type of prayer is necessary for the courts of heaven when you are dealing with strongholds of darkness, or when oppression of witchcraft is involved. The person who is offering this prayer of judgement before the courts of heaven is simply asking God to judge based on the standard of his word. If for instance, a person is going through oppression of witchcraft and the person has prayed and nothing seemed to change. The individual can go before the courts of heaven and ask God to issue a judgement against the person practising the witchcraft.

Many people say that God is a good God why should he judge? Well, even though God is a good God he also has his judgemental aspect.

Which is why the Bible tells us in the book of Romans 11:22:

> *Behold therefore the goodness and severity of God: on them which fell, severity; but toward thee, goodness, if thou continue in his goodness: otherwise thou also shalt be cut off.*

God is a good God. God is also a judgemental God. Even in the dispensation of the New Testament where the Holy Spirit is operating in our lives, God still judges. The Bible tells of the story of how Ananias and Sapphira were on the receiving end of the judgement of God

Acts 5:1-11

> *But a certain man named Ananias, with Sapphira his wife, sold a possession,*

2 And kept back part of the price, his wife also being privy to it, and brought a certain part, and laid it at the apostles' feet.

3 But Peter said, Ananias, why hath Satan filled thine heart to lie to the Holy Ghost, and to keep back part of the price of the land?

4 Whiles it remained, was it not thine own? and after it was sold, was it not in thine own power? why hast thou conceived this thing in thine heart? thou hast not lied unto men, but unto God.

5 And Ananias hearing these words fell down, and gave up the ghost: and great fear came on all them that heard these things.

6 And the young men arose, wound him up, and carried him out, and buried him.
7 And it was about the space of three hours after, when his wife, not knowing what was done, came in.
8 And Peter answered unto her, Tell me whether ye sold the land for so much? And she said, Yea, for so much.
9 Then Peter said unto her, How is it that ye have agreed together to tempt the Spirit of the Lord? behold, the feet of them which have buried thy husband are at the door, and shall carry thee out.
10 Then fell she down straightway at his feet, and yielded up the ghost: and the young men came in, and found her dead, and,

carrying her forth, buried her by her husband.
11 And great fear came upon all the church, and upon as many as heard these things.

The way you pray this kind of prayer is simple, God I am asking you to judge this witchcraft oppression in my life in the name of Jesus. You can also pray in this manner, Holy Father, I have done nothing to this person who is doing witchcraft on me. I am asking you to judge between me and him whether I have done anything wrong to him to justify this continuous oppression that has been released against my life in the name of Jesus.

A scriptural example of praying by judgement is in the book of Luke 18:2-8 when the woman went to the unrighteous judge so that he could judge her enemies:

2 Saying, There was in a city a judge, which feared not God, neither regarded man:

3 And there was a widow in that city; and she came unto him, saying, Avenge me of mine adversary.

4 And he would not for a while: but afterward he said within himself, Though I fear not God, nor regard man;

5 Yet because this widow troubleth me, I will avenge her, lest by her continual coming she weary me.

6 And the Lord said, Hear what the unjust judge saith.

7 And shall not God avenge his own elect, which cry day and night unto him, though he bear long with them?

8 I tell you that he will avenge them speedily. Nevertheless when the Son

*of man cometh, shall he find
faith on the earth?*

Also in the book of Revelation, the Bible tells us about the saints who were praying to God asking him to judge the earth (Revelation 6:10).

By Restraining Order

Praying by restraining order is a type of prayer that seeks to put a permanent end to the works of the devil. I have written extensively about praying by restraining order in Prayers that Open the Courts of Heaven. However, since you are a beginner in the Courts of Heaven prayer, let me explain to you some of the ways you can pray by restraining order in the Courts of Heaven.

When you pray in this manner, you are telling the devil that he has no right to ever attack you again. Or you're telling God that based on the standard of his words in the

Holy Bible, this particular affliction can never rise again the second time. So we are putting an injunction against the works of darkness or when the devil is making use of human agents, you are restraining them in perpetuity.

Job 38:11

> *And said, Hitherto shalt thou come, but no further: and here shall thy proud waves be stayed?*

When you pray before the courts of heaven in this manner, and you are successful a decree will be issued by God to restrain the devil or his agents from afflicting you again. We understand by Scripture that God rules by decree. Which is the reason why he issued a decree against the water and said thus far have you gone, and no further will you go. And that decree is still keeping the waters in their proper place.

Mark 9:25

> *When Jesus saw that the people came running together, he rebuked the foul spirit, saying unto him, Thou dumb and deaf spirit, I charge thee, come out of him, and enter no more into him.*

Jesus demonstrated to us an example of a permanent restraining order against the work of darkness when he was casting out a devil out of the life of a little boy. When he told the devil to come out of him, he added an order, come into him again no more. This represents an example of a restraining order against the devil that was cast out of the life of the boy. I will not go into further details because this is a subject of full discussion in this book, **Restraining Decree Through Courtroom Prayer.**

CHAPTER 8

Beginners Prayers in the Courts of Heaven

The prayers here are not conclusive but examples of how you can use the various methods of praying in the courts of heaven to get your answers. As a beginner, you can use these examples to be able to create your prayer points that you can use to pray in the Courts of Heaven for speedy answers and manifestations. As you begin to gain experience in the Courts of Heaven, praying there won't be difficult.

Intercession prayers in the Courts of Heaven

Reflection

1 Timothy 2:1-2

> *I exhort therefore, that, first of all, supplications, prayers, intercessions, and giving of thanks, be made for all men; 2 For kings, and for all that are in authority; that we may lead a quiet and peaceable life in all godliness and honesty.*

1 Samuel 12:23

> *Moreover as for me, God forbid that I should sin against the Lord in ceasing to pray for you: but I will teach you the good and the right way:*

Holy Father, I commit all of my children before your throne of grace at this hour who have been living contrary to your statutes and getting on the wrong side of the law. I pray Lord that let all the powers of darkness that is holding them bound, lose right now in the name of Jesus.

Heavenly Father, I pray for my husband before your Courts at this hour I destroy all the powers of darkness that have bended his mind towards me so that he treats me contrary to the way he has been treating me, I ask you that let the powers of darkness to lose their grip over his life in the name of Jesus.

Heavenly Father, I commit my wife before your Courts at this hour whatever it is that has bent her mind that is preventing her from being committed to our marriage as she used to do, let that thing loosen its grip over her life in the name of Jesus.

Holy Father, I pray for the stronghold of anger that has remained even after I have fasted, let my bloodline be purged of this anger in the name of Jesus.

Gracious Father, I break every stronghold of diabetes and terminal diseases over the life of my cousins and loved ones in the name of Jesus.

Righteous Father, I commit my colleague at my job before the throne of grace, I am asking you that you intervene in the situation that is causing her to attack me ceaselessly in the name of Jesus.

Holy Father, I come before you to lift my pastor before your throne asking you for divine intervention over his family and the attack that the enemy has brought to their finances in the name of Jesus.

Praying by Petition in the Courts of Heaven

Reflection

1 John 5:14-15

> *And this is the confidence that we have in him, that, if we ask any thing according to his will, he heareth us:*
> *15 And if we know that he hear us, whatsoever we ask, we know that we have the petitions that we desired of him.*

Matthew 7:7

> *Ask, and it shall be given you; seek, and ye shall find; knock, and it shall be opened unto you:*

Holy Father, I ask you that let this yoke of barrenness that has taken over my finances break today in the name of Jesus.

Heavenly Father, you have decreed in your word that I should ask, and I will receive. I make demands for the release of your blessings over my business and the works of my hands in the name of Jesus.

Righteous Father, you have said in your word that the path of the just is as a shining light that will continue to shine until the perfect day. I ask you today that I will never know a better yesterday in every aspect of my life in the name of Jesus.

Gracious Father, I ask you that you surround me with your divine favour so that everywhere I go favour will continue to locate me in the name of Jesus.

Heavenly Father, where I have suffered rejection in my life I ask that you compensate me with double opportunities for all that the rejection has caused me in the name of Jesus.

Holy Father, I asked that you release your banner of divine protection over my life so that I will be shielded from all these oppressions of darkness in the name of Jesus.

Heavenly Father, I asked that you release upon my life your grace of distinction and excellence in the works of my hands so that your grace will make me shine forth in the midst of many in the name of Jesus.

Thank you Holy Father for this petition which you have graciously granted to me in your Courts to you be all the glory and the honour in the name of Jesus.

Praying in the Courts of Heaven by Judgement

Reflection

Luke 18:2-8

> *2 Saying, There was in a city a judge, which feared not God, neither regarded man:*
> *3 And there was a widow in that city; and she came unto him, saying, Avenge me of mine adversary.*

4 And he would not for a while: but afterward he said within himself, Though I fear not God, nor regard man;
5 Yet because this widow troubleth me, I will avenge her, lest by her continual coming she weary me.
6 And the Lord said, Hear what the unjust judge saith.
7 And shall not God avenge his own elect, which cry day and night unto him, though he bear long with them?
8 I tell you that he will avenge them speedily. Nevertheless when the Son of man cometh, shall he find faith on the earth?

Revelation 6:10

And they cried with a loud voice, saying, How long, O

Lord, holy and true, dost thou not judge and avenge our blood on them that dwell on the earth?

Heavenly Father, I have done nothing to this person (mention the name of the person that is attacking you with witchcraft if you know) who has been using witchcraft attack to me and my family, I ask you that you judge between me and the person (mention the name again if the person is known to you) let the person be judge according to the standard of your word in the name of Jesus.

Holy Father, let your judgemental fire fall on every voodoo priest, high priest, and Priestess that have been attacking me in the name of Jesus.

Gracious Father, I ask that you judge every gatekeeper of darkness in my family that is currently enforcing generational curses in the name of Jesus.

Heavenly Father, every agent of darkness that is currently looking at me with an evil eye, let your judgemental fire blind that eye in the name of Jesus.

Holy Father, you have said in your word that you are a consuming fire I pray that you consume to ashes in your righteous judgement every evil altar that has been set up in my name in the name of Jesus.

Gracious Father, every man or woman that has been using that altar to bring affliction to me, let your judgement come upon them now in the name of Jesus.

Righteous Father, every form of seasonal failure that we have been experiencing in our family which is as a result of the work of the spirit of failure, I decree your judgemental fire upon the spirit in the name of Jesus.

Holy Father, every devil that is assigned to my family to prevent the purpose for which you have predestinated for my family from coming to pass, let your fire of judgement come upon the devil right now in the name of Jesus.

Thank you Holy Father for the judgement which you have released from your Courts to you be all the glory forever in the name of Jesus.

Praying in the Courts of Heaven by Restraining Order

Reflection

Mark 9:25

> *When Jesus saw that the people came running together, he rebuked the foul spirit, saying unto him, Thou dumb and deaf spirit, I charge thee, come out of*

*him, and enter no more into
him.*

Proverbs 8:15

*By me kings reign, and
princes decree justice.*

Holy Father, every arrow of darkness that has been fired against my health, those arrows are restrained from reaching me in the name of Jesus.

Heavenly Father, every arrow of darkness that has been fired against my finances, by the order of your Courts those arrows of darkness are restrained from reaching me in the name of Jesus.

Gracious Father, every arrow of division that has been fired against my family, those arrows are restrained from reaching us by the power in the name of Jesus.

Holy Father, the attacks of the kingdom of darkness against my marriage are restrained by the blood of Jesus.

Heavenly Father, whatever attacks that the enemy has planted against my children, those attacks are restrained from taking effect in their lives in the name of Jesus.

Righteous Father, whatever weapon the enemy has planted against my husband that weapon is ordered destroyed and ineffective against him in the name of Jesus.

Thank you Holy Father for the restraining order which you have granted against the devil and his agents to you be all the glory and the honour in the name of Jesus.

Important Decision

If you are reading this book and you are not saved, pray this prayer after me:

Lord Jesus, I come before you today. I give you my heart. I give you my all. Come into my life. Become my Lord and saviour. Deliver me from the power of sin. Help me to live for you forever, in Jesus name.

Our Books

1.   Restraining Decrees through Courtroom Prayers: Courts of Heaven Orders for Victory & Breakthroughs

2.   Python Spirit: Complete Deliverance from the Python Spirit with Powerful Prayers

3.   The Courts of Heaven: Prayers that Open the Courts of Heaven for Healing and Deliverance

4.   Powerful Prayers for Your Adult Children: How to Pray for Your Children and Secure their Future

5.   Praying for My Future Husband:How to Pray for Your Husband and Enjoy A Godly Marriage

6.   Praying God's Promises to Reality: Simple Ways of Praying the Promises of God for Victory & Breakthrough

7.   God Wants You Protected From Disease

8.   Under His Divine Protection

9.   7 Day Fasting Challenge That Will Change Your Life Forever: 7 Powerful Prayers to Pray in 7 Days

10.   Praying Through the Book of Psalms for Financial Miracle: The Financial Miracle Prayer for Breakthrough

11.   Burning Evil Garments: Prayers That Destroy Evil Garments, Deliverance, Breakthroughs And God's Favour Into Your Life

12.   30 Days with the Holy Spirit: Powerful Prayers and Devotional for Personal Connection with the Holy Spirit and Be His Friend

13.   Breaking Evil Altars: Prayers, Decrees, Declarations for Dismantling Evil Altars

14.   How to see the Supernatural: Powerful Prayers that open the Unseen Realm

15.   Breaking the Spell of Disfavour: Prayers Declarations and Decrees

16.   Deliverance from Shame and Reproach: Prayers, Declarations for Victory

17.   Prayers that Destroy Infirmities & Diseases: Powerful Prayers that bring Healing to the Sick

18.   Courtroom Prayers: Prayers And Declarations in the Courts of Heaven For Victory, Breakthrough, and Deliverance (Free E-Book

19.   How to make the Holy Ghost Your Closest Friend (Book 2) (Free-Ebook)

20.   The Keys to Fervent Prayer: The Prayer Warrior Guide to Praying Always

21.   Interpretation of Tongues: Be Filled with the Spirit, Unlock Speaking in Tongues & Know What You Are Praying

22.   Deliverance from negative Dreams and Nightmares by Force

23.   How to Build a Life of Personal Devotion to God (Free-Ebook)

24.   The Holy Spirit Friendship Manual: How to make the Holy Ghost Your Close Friend (Free-Ebook)

34. Guide to Effective Fasting and Praying: A Way of Fasting And Prayers That Guarantee Results

Prayer

Let us know about your prayer needs as our team add you to our prayer list and intercede fervently on your behalf.

Also, check our blog for Holy Ghost inspired content.

www.thetentofglory.com

I would love to hear from you how our ministry and our books have blessed you. Write to us at

pius@thetentofglory.com